T0327282

SIGHTSEER

CYNTHIA MARIE HOFFMAN

SIGHTSEER

WINNER OF THE 2010 LEXI RUDNITSKY FIRST BOOK PRIZE IN POETRY

A KAREN & MICHAEL BRAZILLER BOOK

PERSEA BOOKS / NEW YORK

Copyright © 2011 by Cynthia Marie Hoffman

All rights reserved. No part of this may be reproduced or transmitted in any form or by any means, electronic or mechanical, including photocopy, recording, or any information storage and retrieval system, without prior permission in writing from the publisher. Request for permission to reprint or make copies, and for any other information, should be addressed to the publisher:

Persea Books, Inc.
853 Broadway
New York, NY 10003

Library of Congress Cataloging-in-Publication Data
Hoffman, Cynthia Marie.
Sightseer / Cynthia Marie Hoffman. — 1st ed.
          p. cm.
"A Karen & Michael Braziller book."
"Winner of the 2010 Lexi Rudnitsky first book prize in poetry."
ISBN 978-0-89255-368-6 (original trade pbk. : alk. paper)
1. Europe — Description and travel — Poetry. I. Title.
PS3608.O47765S54 2011
811'.6 — dc22
                    2010048437

Designed by Rita Lascaro

FIRST EDITION

Printed in the United States of America

Contents

SIGHTSEER

DEAR FLUORESCENT PINK
JUMBO FINGER STARFISH,

You are the most horrendous thing I have ever seen.
You alone are the one magnificent and irrefutable
symbol of capitalism, of everything that is wrong with tourism.
But what am I saying already? I love you. Just look at

those warts! That obscenely speckled crimson flush!
You have no front, no back; you can move in any direction
without turning around. Your gonads are in your
arms, for Christ's sake. Who wouldn't want to take you home?

I paid the three-fifty in cash. The woman bound you in bread paper
and I paraded down the main street with my plastic-
handled shopping bag with the sharp silhouette of a steamboat
and in all caps: PROVINCETOWN.

Starfish, I am the idiot tourist who believes you washed ashore
in a wreck of starfish in Provincetown, you changed
from embryo to blastula to larva in Provincetown, gathered
Provincetown mussels and shore worms into your belly.

So what? So what if you were shipped from the Philippines?
If we've all been duped out of our three-fifty cash?
You are the radial array of wharfs all around the peninsula,
the fluttering jazz hands of the Provincetown Cabaret.

I have been entranced by your spectacle.
I have contributed to the commoditization of the natural world.
I have displaced the locals with my outside capital.
What I am trying to say is that I am a bad person.

I am a bad person for the buzz I got off
unwrapping you back in my hotel in private. For having lifted you
out of your wooden bin in the first place, thinking I was saving you,
when really I was propagating your species.

Both of us disgust me. My corrupt fingertips
stink of your death. That vile stench of beach rot, fungus,
wet dog. I can't believe I put my bare skin on you. But
I don't know what I'm saying. You are a symbol

of immortality. Your hard carcass laughs
at the brief flickering of my life, the human need to make history.
The guarantee that you will leave your mark on this earth
is written into your own body. *Asteroidea prospera*.

Lucky starfish. Don't ever leave me.

GOOD JESUS, GOOD DOG

It is not that I have come here to pray, repent whatever
wicked things I've done before an altar frothing with goldleaf.
Nor is it my design to rub holes through the knees of my

Easter dress as I crawl the stairs to the sanctuary.
Nor do I present my tongue to the fountains of Faith,
Hope, and Chastity. Scarcely a pilgrim, I did not presume

to receive an usher in the form of a white mutt. And yet,
rejoice! that tail of yours has appeared, a mislaid wing
that rocks your haunches, launches you up the stairs

more a helicopter than an angel—not that I believe you are either.
We climb together the terraced corridors of the Fourteen
Stations of the Cross, to the *Bom Jesus*, the Good Jesus.

And at each of the fourteen life-sized Terracotta Christs, you sit, stay
time enough to permit my requisite gawking. You are not surprised
by my pockets empty of flowers, my camera a prayer bead

I raise to my face. And why should this seem strange to you?
You can only glimpse inside the Cathedral lit up with worship
before the steel toe drives you out the door. When you will not go home

to soaked lamb's leg dotted with olives, Sunday spinach and cheese pie,
what use have you for candles and marble tile? You are always a penitent
on your short legs, chafing your shabby belly on the stairs,

your shoulder stained with mange. Yet your floppy ears betray you,
a lost dog in the one place God has charted out for you,
where daily He sends visitors who pull crackers from their bags,

who are willing, as I am, to kneel and rub your ears, take a mite
away in my palm. Few receive their calling as clearly as you.
With your callused paws you read these steps,

the mosaic tile haloed with moss, better than any man
who might walk the way of the three virtues
barefoot, his sandals hooked onto his thumb.

Little attendant, guide me to the flight of stairs
where into the stone of each landing is written
good dog, good dog, good dog.

DEAR ALEXANDER NEVSKY,

Do you know what things they've said
about you since you died at Gorodets?
They say as you lay in the open
casket, your fist uncurled like a morning glory.
This alone is no call for alarm;
it's a common thing for cadavers
to interrupt their own autopsy
by sitting up and spilling the heart and spleen
into their laps. But legend has it
your palm clasped shut again
when the scroll, on which your burial prayer
was written, was laid in it. They made you a saint
and granted you a street for this,
the longest and widest in Petersburg.

It's from here that I write you this letter, admitting
I've walked the Nevsky Prospekt for seven days
and haven't thought about you once, until now.
I'm not ashamed to say it. Instead,
I've thought only of Akhmatova, how she
too walked here, how down from the Fontanka
she dragged her sullen profile on the palace wall,
nose like a broken wing. I believe in the poet
who sits in a chair worn through to the springs,
who stands at Kresty prison with an armful of bread,

who always packs her nitroglycerin tablets in her purse
and dies anyway.
Nevsky, namesake of asphalt, saint
of the timely convulsion, pray for me.

BURNING PAPER IN LAZARUS CEMETERY

The woman who works in the cemetery in her blue smock
bends to pick a scrap of paper from the earth
and drop it in the barrel as a god would drop
a bird into a sputtering volcano. A white smoke
rises and disappears. All around her,
crosses are popping up like crooked weeds.
Listen to the little river swish
along the walls of the canal. Nearby, a fresh grave
is plump with flowers, a mound like a dozen girls
fainted in their ruffled party skirts. What better place
to be set into the ground? The trees
lower long necks to the water, their many flat faces
nodding at their own reflections. The woman bends.
Another bird is lit afire.

DEAR SUNSET, JULY 12TH,

You put all the palaces and golden
spires in Petersburg to shame

and you know it. You turn St. Isaac's Cathedral
into a giant crouching bullfrog.

Take as evidence the colossal
gilded wart on its head

where inside sits the wooden cupola
inside the wooden cupola

like a Russian matryoshka doll
painted by an old man who climbed

its stairs, stamping Virgin Mary
blue on the wall with his palms. Yes,

I meant what I said about the bullfrog
with dolls in its head, and if it sounds extraordinary,

it is. You move too fast,
you make me want to leap

up and run after you
the length of the Neva

over all five hundred bridges
all the way to the Gulf of Finland.

IDIOT GREEN SALAD

Tell me the story of the mercury gilding of the dome
at St. Isaac's Cathedral, and do you remember the number
of people who died and whether the vapors

swayed with faintly human expression as they rose.
The 400 kilograms of real gold, 4 bell towers, 40 tons of marble, 40,000 workers,
40 years' construction. Each of the workers' two hands, one pressed to the cold

140-ton red granite column, the other to his heaving chest.
Can you give me directions to the Café Idiot? I have looked
forward to lettuce, cucumber, tomato, orange, avocado, and nut.

How many gallons of gray paint were necessary to hide
the gold from the Nazis. Whether the men
dropped off the dome or collapsed later in their homes. Whether it burned.

If at night, at the sink, the bright trail of blood seeping to the drain
startled them one by one. Whether the workers
wandered the cathedral, lost. If the shimmering

dome can be seen from the shores of the Neva Bay. Dostoyevsky
was pardoned at the execution scaffold, a sword
broken over his head. If the spirit is roused

by the sight of its godly shimmering. After
the herring in spicy sauce, the icefruit cools your tongue.
Whether their hands shook. Whether it was worth it.

TOMB

Because the wrought iron gates were so awkwardly spread—
like a dead crow's wings unhinged in the useless air—
I begged no invitation passing through them.

I was not your first visitor. Nor were the spiders
resting atop their webs like chachkas on a corner shelf,
nor the water trickling through the concrete dome.

Nor the gardener whose clippers dripped
with dandelion milk. The Star of David was plucked
of its stained glass, save for one point gesturing to the sky.

The first to slide the stone from your face and break apart your jaw
was not your last, though you had no flash of gold to give.
Marie Pohlova, have you begun to take pleasure in these visits?

What sorry company I was, offering no warmth from my hurried hand.
Nor could we exchange, for I was frightened and my greed of a different kind,
the affection a thief shares with the dead, palm passing over chest

long since bared of jewels. This photograph was all I wanted to take.
And I knew that having no way to speak up or strike at my ankle
with your bony hand, you would let me have it. Let me lean at the little stairway,

point my camera toward the ceiling, where
the peeling paint is rolled tight as a flock of fingers
forsaken by the Pohlovas—your sister, your father—as they

rose from their caskets and scraped their way through to the heavens.
Measly recompense it is, Marie, letting me walk away
with the rusted rails imprinted at my hip, a marked woman.

SANTUARI DE SANT SALVADOR

Even from the road, where sheep are scattered
across the valley with their noses plunged to the bristled turf,
the sanctuary gleams like a spindle of gauze
touched to the forehead of the mountain.

And once inside, more brilliant still the whitewashed
walls, the pristine crystal chandelier, the alabaster altarpiece
a sheet of plaited wings on which the cherubs rest their
sleepy golden heads. One-hundred-ninety years

have sloughed away the ashes of the Black Death,
driven the moaning lazaretto to the ground, and raised
this hall in its place, bright and clean. Only a dark
corner persists in remembrance. I was rapt by light

and could not see the stair below me sunken into
shadow by a century's promenade of monks.
And even as it brought me to my knees, bone
sounding a single clap upon the stone,

there was nothing but light, the rose window
a brilliant whorl of petals set to spinning. And then
outside, in the dizzying height, I stood at the foot of Christ
the King, His arm extended in blessing. I thought

I could hear the squeak of a blade of grass
sliding against the ivory spire of a tooth.
Though it was impossible to distinguish
a single sheep grazing in the distance.

SHEEPIFICATION

Since men have shepherded this flock with cursive staff in hand
and harvested your wrinkled skins for parchment,
centuries have passed their tired slump into these mountains.

Yet tirelessly still you write the verse of this valley
in a crimped and woolly scrawl. Though surely you know, wise ram,
you are marked by the horned *e*'s at your cheeks, the pitch of your sheep bell

that with each nod of your grazing head rings your subservience
throughout the grass and leafy spurge. Master Poet, heralded
for the alchemy that makes Choice carcass from forage alone,

makes milk and hoops of cheese, boiled wool spun into sweaters
to warm the fisherman's arms as he raises them over the deck
and releases the net to the sea. No one is reading your poem

in which I make my brief appearance late in the afternoon's fifth stanza
as a dim moon, opening and closing her eyes, emerging from a window
in the red planet's shadowy orbit charging down the road.

Bless the sheep for whom night is more than the plaster ceiling,
the clicking whir of the ceiling fan. The sheep who would never
write the mountains as the hips and breasts of lovers. Who write

instead mountains as they glimpse them over chilled shoulders
driven out the barn door once a year: the lumpy
disheveled heaps fleeced from their backs. This loss is written

into the sweater folded deep in a drawer, cedar block on its chest,
the tangled fringe of the afghan tossed to the foot of the bed.
What does a sheep know of breasts? Bless the sheep.

DEAR REMU'H SYNAGOGUE,

You are the miraculous synagogue of Krakow,
little white thing at the end of the road.
How did you swallow the 70,000 prayers, your belly
full of fringed shawls, the clasping and unclasping of palms?
The most immaculate walls in the walled city.
How did you live out the war?
                        Remember,
when I come to your doorway with my heavy camera
beating at my hip, you have seen worse.
Let me lift it; I'm proud
of how cheap a roll of film is in the Jewish quarter.
Let me glide past the man who stands with his wife
at the folding table with the china tea saucer of coins.
He is gray, but tireless. Look how he leaps
in the nick of time, arm in the air,
aiming the flimsy wing of a skull cap
at the back of a bald man's head, so that the fear
of heaven may be upon him.
                    Look at this man:
a head of hair like my father's, like the Vistula River
stirring with little wakes the shape of fins.
It's been more than fifty years and still
he funnels sand into his shoes to remember.
And now he sweeps out his long arm
as if there were a door in the air
that he was opening for me,
and says (yes, says it in English)

Come in, come in.
            These are the five reasons
I did not right then leave him all the money I had:
I cannot repeat a single name set to heart in the barracks.
With my own hands I have laid flowers on a grave.
I could not say the Kaddish to save him. Tonight
I will pass the Polish border in my sleep. I go
through the synagogue with my hair
flailing about my neck.
            Out back,
the rows of Renaissance tombstones
are saved under flat, sheet iron hats. On their shoulders
they balance a small collection of stones
left behind by visitors.
These are the eyes the dead look out from
thinking *ignorant girl.*
            I am not ashamed
that I photographed intricate writing
I cannot read. Or that I rolled my pant legs
when the sun shot through the trees,
put my elbow on one of those iron sheets
and thought of where I could get a meal.
I take none of it back. But I ask you now,
in place of the coins I'd already spent on postcards,
to deliver from me
            this one confession:

Forgive me, old man,

for not having caught a bus into Auschwitz

though there are ten buses per day

turning the 64 kilometers. I hear

I can hire a foreign-language

guide at the information desk.

There's a cheap self-service Bar

Smak facing the car park.

I could have become your daughter.

                                     Don't miss

going to the top of the entrance gate

for the view.

DEAR HERZEN INN,

Don't laugh at me. From my window
looking out upon the courtyard, I can see
an abandoned rusted bathtub
and I want to lie down in it. For days
no one has come into the square
with a wooden cart. I say it is there
for the taking. After a rain, when the dogs come
loping with their giant tongues
hanging neat as guest towels,
I will be the pearl in your trough. Herzen,
the Kasansky Cathedral pays no attention;
its dome sits resolute as the back of a father's
bald head. It is as if all of St. Petersburg
has turned its back on me. After a rain,
it would be easy to hold my breath
at the bottom of the tub, letting my hair
drift to the top and fan out like a lily pad,
surprisingly easy to shoot my arm out of the water
just as the dogs lean in to drink, and
rip the tongues from their jowls in one swift snap.
Herzen, I have not slept. I want to sleep.

IN PUSHKIN PARK, AN OLD WOMAN

drinks milk on a bench near the bushes and kicks
at the dust. The dust disappears into a hole in her shoe
as a crowd is shuffled through the door of a train. Her cane

rests. When she drinks, the whiskers on her chin scratch
the cardboard carton. What is their sound? A mouse
in the night, dragging its toenails inside the wall. Tourists come

with their cameras to Pushkin's statue, to pose as he poses, stately,
right palm toward the sky. Like an impatient child,
the wind tugs at their coats. The old woman swallows.

A young woman is playing hide and seek with her
children. She runs to Pushkin, rests her head against her wrist,
counts in Japanese. The children climb into the bushes. She runs

through the park calling their names, and the bushes come alive
with funny little birdsong. The White Nights are nearly over.
Beneath the old woman, the bench has begun to gather up

its curls of paint, which have labored long in their peeling,
readying themselves as if momentarily the heavens
would call her into them, as if the curls, worn and tired,

would ascend with her at last. They hitch
themselves to the folds of her long skirt. They tremble now
in anticipation. The children huddling in the bush.

THE HEART OF SINTRA

To see the world and leave out Sintra
is to go blind about.
　　　　　—*Spanish proverb*

At the heart of Sintra, at the Royal Palace,
a pair of enormous chimneys surges into the sky
like ravenous birds thrusting their hairless necks
from a nest of stone woven by Moors and kings.

Nearby, high above the cobbles, a woman
whose hair is white and thin as a bonnet of lace
draws open her shutters. The pigeons are already
assembling in their hustling, flapping manner, slapping their dry
orange feet along the roof. The air in the alley is awhirl.

Her hand disappears into a heavy sack and returns
to the sill heaped with black and golden corn. Who is shy
in the presence of this delicate palm, pale as the apartment's
peach façade from which each day, alleluia, it emerges?
Not the feathers which bear the pigeon upon the air,
the pointed beak that dips into the human cup.

When the woman raises her head, she finds me
on the balcony of my hotel, and watching me, she lifts
her hand to stroke the slick airy creature, where deep inside
thrums the fiery current of its heart. From here,
her face is blurred by the flock's eager

swirl of wings, as if she were the secret axis
upon which all winged things turn, the pocket of air
at the core of a knot of birds. Even the frescoed swans
and magpies who dignify the palace halls. Even
the giant chimneys clamoring toward the empty sky.

ISLAND OF DONAN CASTLE

> The traditional account related how the raid, perhaps carried out by Vikings,
> had been organized by a local woman who had lost her grazing rights
> when the monks had taken over the island.
> —Butler's Lives of the Saints

In the distance which belittles your generous
cluster of stone and chimneys, your silhouette is something
tenuously human. Your bare back, your body gathered

tightly about your heart. A bridge across the water
like the limb of a prisoner on the stretching rack, hauntingly thin.
Everyone says how beautiful you are. Even the sea

flutters around you and murmurs a language of cold and deep. It is true
they would toss a prisoner from your roof, and if he could swim to land
he would live. Once you were nothing but a little monk's cell

with a little hooded monk huddling inside. Once you sat for two-hundred years
crumbling against the sky, and the clouds passed through your deepest parts
where until then, only certain men had passed in nightdress.

Was it for the sheep Saint Donan's head was unfastened by the sword?
Such a delicate puff of a thing, a sheep. The mercurial eye,
and the form of a holy man gliding across its surface

as a leaf rides the bend in a stream and is gone. The invaders
held their three-pound swords glinting in the bright air until the celebration
of the sacrament inside the church was finished. It was Saint Donan

who saw them climb the shore and made them wait, who led
his brothers out the door to save the dimness of the holy wooden chamber
the pollution of their deaths, and as they marched, the sunlight

rimmed their hoods in gold. And then it was fifty-one monks' heads
or fifty-three depending on the account and counting the head of Donan.
This was the year 617. A curious silence swept over the island like a great wind

hurled into motion by the blood that shoves forth from its human body
and displaces the air around it. And then, the gardens began to receive
a roving pattern of wing-shaped hooves. The lacy yarrow's leaves

quivered at the muzzle's touch. A turnip popped from the earth
flashed its startling red skins. It might have been 618. It is not clear
why they have been classified martyrs. No prisoner

ever survived the swim across the roiling underbelly of the Scottish Lochs.
Even now the chills are swirling up your spiral staircase and into
your bedroom which is said to be haunted. And in the evenings,

when the moonlight electrifies the swells in the water all around you,
it is Saint Donan's face which bobs to the surface, his pointed beard intact.
And the sheep sleep soundly upon the hill, fat and luminous.

IN THE CEMETERY,
THE LIKENESS OF JESUS

hovers at the tomb like a bronze bird,
wings outstretched but stripped of feather.
Neither can he rise to the trees, let loose
the nail from his foot, nor tumble to the ground
and lie in a puff of dust.

A wild coil of vine has clambered all over this wall,
across the thighs, the bare bird bones of Jesus,
and slung itself across his torso like the sash
of a guard who keeps the dead from passing
into the careless onrush of the living.

The buds are a gathering of lips, each one now
a kiss in the Czech language. But what are you going to do
when the leaves have opened upon your eyes?
When the rustling of the leaves is louder than a scarf
tossed into your face by the wind?
When finally you are nothing but a clump of green?

RAIN AT THE DRESDNER FRAUENKIRCHE

For many years the stones were lifted from the heap
and set upon a shelf like bits of seashell. Rows of shelves.
A hundred shelves. A chunk of coiling spire.
Lucky hulking boulder. A chip, a meager chip, which bears
the strenuous curvature of an arch.

Nearby, a man attends his patient cart beneath a broad umbrella
where before him, spread upon a tray, a whimsical
zoology of wooden toys, each no bigger than a finger
and bright as a lump of candy.

They are push-button puppets, what the man is selling. Plunge the button
and the giraffe, or perhaps it is a donkey, or an elephant, monkey, dog,
human collapses.

What is one thousand degrees Celsius? Even the sandstone
pillars that glowed like hot pokers cannot say what it is.
Even the distinctive stone bell that popped like a grape.

It is only when the puppet falls that the thread between its joints
becomes visible. I select one from the tray, though I know
the toys are Swiss and this is Germany. I know what country I am in.

The Dresdner Frauenkirche is a Lutheran church, and I was baptized
Lutheran, with an understanding of the heritable sin, the root
and fountainhead of all sins.

Already the rows of catalogued debris are taking shape as pews,
the stones themselves heads bowed in worship. See how the stone
is given back its place on the wall.

How will they know how to rebuild the oak doors? Now they're thank-
ful for the throngs of people who posed for portraits in the light
of their giant flash bulbs. The bride's veil like a luminous jellyfish.

Even the tourists with their heavy hands upon their children's shoulders
are now of use. Each of the children's eyes a glass marble
in which a wisp of a shadow is suspended. In the 1930s,
it was the sin of what hadn't happened yet. Today,
it is the sin of what has already passed.

And look, the great golden cross, which once
topped the dome that pummeled the earth
like a six-thousand pound stormcloud breaking,
endures, though its twisted arms
seem to me now flimsy, nothing more than seaweed
ensnarled in a sweeping current. I am sorry.

This is the game. Release the button
and it springs again to life with perfect form.

I come here. The rubber wheels of the cart are a disappointment.

I buy a dark braided roll by pointing at it through the glass.

I leap over the puddles. Am I not a pilgrim?

Is it because of my waterproof jacket? I am not saying I am not

American. The miniature giraffe falls limp

by the force of my thumb.

PAS DE DEUX

As if she had reached the edge of the earth, the point
closest to the sky, the black cat reclines atop the wall
of the burned house, which stretches like a balance beam
across the alley, and flashes her red tongue.

Now merely a heap, out of which a garden has slowly come to pass,
imagine here the roof that was: orderly, elegant shingles
buoyed in the final moments before the collapse
like the frills of a ballerina's skirt as she is lifted by her partner.

Only the cat acknowledges with a fluttering of whiskers
what once had been. At times, imparts the warmth of her rumbling body.

Vines dangle where once a woman rubbed her hands
on a cloth, the bedroom where a man's silk tie
slipped from the doorknob. A peel of blue paint
remains. A door opens onto the sky. The wind touches them.

Here a fresh bundle of moss erupts. Weeds sway
their spindly arms. New grasses stand tall as they can,
shoving amongst themselves for a glimpse
into a shard of mirror. And each night,

as if in remembrance, embers stir and fizzle into the sky.
A star is something that happened many years ago.

GAUDÍ'S CANDELABRA

> Who knows if we have given this diploma to a madman or a genius.
> Time will tell.
>   —*Elies Rogent, upon signing the title of Architect for Antoni Gaudí*

As the long afternoon passes through Palma Cathedral,
radiant stipples of light descend the octagonal pillars and slip
to the floor, cross the golden limestone walls

to touch upon the walnut stalls where the choir strikes
a harmony of tones as clear as if it were a belfry
clapped by the human spirit, and mark the stair where once

or twice the man they called God's Architect rested
his rheumatic joints, where the tatters of his trousers
brushed the floor. Gaudí's candelabra

hovers like a fiery halo high above the nave. And even higher
levitates his airy Crown of Thorns which waits, unfinished,
as if the body of the savior itself would advance from the altar

and step into place beneath it, forehead to the chilled ring.
He is an unfinished man. Across the Mediterranean to Barcelona,
only eight of the twelve towers for the Apostles, four

for the Evangelists, for the Virgin Mary and for Jesus Christ
thrust their spindled arms into the sky. The gaping hole
between them is an open mouth that receives the sacrament—

a white puff of cloud that passes into it at dusk—
on behalf of the bones encrypted beneath. And here, on the island
of Mallorca, the crown of Jesus resolutely clings to its scraps

of colored tile and iron. The road to sainthood is long.
Seated in the pews, aren't we scarcely flecks of dust in this magnificent
kaleidoscope against which the dazzling eye of God is pressed?

THE POTTED FERNS GATHER

in the Renaissance courtyard close to the port at Palma
and chatter amongst themselves in some exclusive discourse
of green, of saucer bowls shimmering with water.
What wouldn't we give to divine the mouthless
utterances of those who beat their many
pointed tongues upon the air? The moss
rises from its lowly latticework among the cobbles
to better hear them. I clutch the iron gate but nothing
comes to me, save the shushing
vault of the colonnade. The marble chills me.
Who holds the key? A column stands
at attention, close enough to hear
the wind brush upon the grand staircase like a maiden
in her fluttering dress and weave among the rippling crowd.
How many green hands applaud?
Whose shoulders bounce in the shadows? Let me in!
Even the tops of the marble pillars are bursting into flower.

IN DRESDEN, A WALL WITHOUT A HOUSE

persists as if it has been 1945 for fifty years,
as if the carriage draws near with its sooty mound.

A girl clutches her father's coattail as they hurry past.
She turns to look at me. What can I say to her?

Every perfect orange brick is a bandage spread across
an open wound the organs have already tumbled out of.

The piano strings have snapped. In the closet, the dresses
have shriveled and slipped from their hangers through the floor.

The rug has lifted into the air and for a moment
hovered there before releasing its ashes into the street.

No one is screaming today. The sky is blank. In the windows,
three stories high, six white ghosts stand at attention. Sparrows

fly directly through their hearts. Nearby, the clock tower
has a new golden face. There is a chill in the air.

It is not necessary to run.

IN THE RUSSIAN GRAVEYARD, A SQUIRREL

stands at attention, flashing his white chest. Here we are,
the tourist and the small red creature

that skitters along the path leftright, and into
the leaves, a sound like a small crackling fire. The impassive

sky hangs in the trees. We are surrounded by concrete:
concrete grave beds bursting with little stabbing leaves,

this concrete wall and on the other side, street, apartments.
Look, he overturns a nut, spins it with his slender toes

as a god spins a planet, smooth, round, dark.
He picks at the leaves. This one, long and curling,

the ear of my sister's horse. This one, golden.
He takes them into his mouth and up, ears pointing, makes

a bed in the sky. What interests a squirrel?
Acorns, hazelnuts, chestnuts, beech flowers.

He stands, wrists slack against his body,
the opposite of prayer. The opposite of the dead.

DEAR ATHASSEL PRIORY,

You were only an infant
at the age of 247 years;
there was no way for you
to defend yourself. The whole world
understands this. So why
should you be ashamed
that all that remains are your jagged
stone teeth, your jaw unhinged in terror?

You should be proud. I walked
the five thin miles on a road
like a tightrope from Cashel
to cross your handsome portcullis
gateway, to climb the stairs
into the Irish fog. The sun
remembers the six o'clock vespers
and every evening impales itself
on the western wall of your church
sharp as an arrowhead. You see?

No one forgets you. Even the Suir River,
now little more than a creek,
still flaps with salmon and trout.
And the grass sweetening
in your cemetery is tended by
the cows who amble through the cloister,
their knees blackened from kneeling in mud,

and swat their tails at the jackdaws
nesting in the arcade. You are more protected
now than you have ever been. A cow's eyes
are clearer than anyone gives them credit for.

And even if hundreds of years ago
their ancestors were grazing these fields
when the flames
burst through your stained glass,
if they saw the docile Augustinian
monks running from the sacristy,
flinging themselves in the river,
leaping over the berry bushes,
bunching their robes up over
their bare legs, and falling down
to press their blisters into the cool grass
contaminated with the secular world,
the cows will never tell a soul.

THIS IS PRAGUE

City of the castle, Death turning over the hourglass,
man rising from mud raked out of the Vltava river.

Yes, the hill of gravestones swelling like a blister pushing out a fingernail.
Yes, the plump Town Hall stuffed into her fading pink housedress.

This tower, crumbling, tangled in scaffolding as if
spiders scaled the cobblestones on their giant wooden legs.

Someone has written something on the wall in English.
The clock with its crooked mustache.

A man is smoothing a crumpled map across his lap,
and the sound of so many tiny folds popping open

is a rainstorm rushing over the Eastern Bloc.
And look, children crouching on the cracks

in the city streets with a little coin,
digging out the shadow of Kafka.

CHIPPING YELLOW WALL

At the edge of the square, a girl is listening
to the chink of coins in her grandmother's apron,
the ripple of the giant blue umbrella hoisted into the wind.
The girl unhinges her little tin box.

Her grandmother lowers loose breasts
over the refrigerated cart, fishes a soda from the ice
for a man whose copper spills from a pouch in his belt,
whose sweatshirt boasts *Poland* in fine embroidered cursive.

The girl scatters mints from the tin into the street, white and sudden
as a mouthful of teeth. She crouches, gathers flakes of gold
from the sidewalk, which the wall bestows upon her
behind her grandmother's back. My shadow

passes over her. And in the bell tower, the trumpet of the Virgin
Mary throws its hourly fit. Funny tourist I must make
with my back to the hurling fountain, the grand
arches of Cloth Hall, raising my long crystal eye

toward some anonymous decaying wall. The girl snaps shut
her tin of brittle currency. What can we know of history?
The clouds are boxcars chugging out of the station
and the sun behind them a lamppost

flickering. The umbrella flashes PEPSI! PEPSI! PEPSI!
across anything in its shade. The pale cheeks of the girl.
The mutterings of an old babushka slitting her knuckles on ice.
An account of a blue silhouette standing guard

as a man shovels a trench out of the dirt beneath his own feet,
a flash of sunlight as the blue silhouette cocks his head,
aims the rifle. I have seen a rifle like that on television.
I tell the old woman *yes, yes* the uniform with pips and silver braid,

black patent leather chin strap. The girl has seen the photograph
her grandmother carries, her grandfather's huge nostrils, beard
wound tight into springs. *Tak, tak* she says because each time
the brittle paper is drawn out into the light, there is his gaze

which seems to have looked, to be still looking
out from his pose on the wooden stool
past the cameraman's balding head, past the iron window
casements slung with leafy vines and into the cobbled streets,

past yellow apartments, red apartments, cream apartments
into the future in which moments after his body topples
into a grave, it is toppled upon by the shovel he used to dig it,
and further into the future to the end of the road

at the edge of this square where his wife has grown old
pushing her cart of soda. But that is all. Nothing else.
What is it possible to know? I bought the Pepsi and I drank it
and it was refreshing. It was a beautiful day.

TRIPE EATER

At the port, where rabelo boats are rich with barrels of wine,
it is as if a drunken jester tossed his shoes into the River Douro.
A tabby wriggles from an overturned skiff. Stub-tailed beggar,

your mewling would not have me indulge poetry. Yet
your ribs rub my calf like a xylophone's keys. What bone
can I extend to your whiskers to redeem myself,

my enchanted view of your city? I can only
scratch your hollow belly, in which resonates
the mallet-strike of aged plaster crumbling to the street,

tiles plunking the steps from the church's mosaic façade,
the swish of thread-bare rugs bobbing on the laundry line
and popping a clothespin to the bricks.

Behind lace curtains, a woman peels the apron from her skirt.
The house is dark. On the sill, the potted narcissus glows.
She pulls her chair to the table, leans over a dish

of steaming honeycomb tripe. What use is a metaphor
that cannot fill even an alley cat's tiny stomach?
The calf's hoof rests in the ladle.

TRANSVERBERATION OF THE HEART

> In a small reliquary (9.30am-1.30pm & 3.30-7.30pm; free),
> beside the gift shop, are memorials of Teresa's life,
> including not only her rosary beads, but one of the fingers
> she used to count them with.
> —Spain: The Rough Guide

> I could move, I think, only one finger of my right hand.
> —*St. Teresa of Avila*

It was not like standing before the figure of Saint Teresa
rendered in marble, in which her Carmelite habit
tumbles luxuriously and eternally to the floor
and the cherub's creamy cheeks flush as he withdraws
his golden spear. Here, in the cluttered reliquary,
in the midst of rose petals once touched to her body,
the sole of her sandal like a dry panting tongue,
a vial of her blood no bigger than a thimble
housed in the miniature bust of a nun
from which the golden rays of godliness and light radiate,
a hole where her heart would have been, it was forbidden
to draw the camera from my bag like a sleeping
squirrel curled tight around the precious nut
in which already were sealed the ghostly forms
of the Basilica's bells rocking back and forth
in the tower's airy skull, the iron
gate of the Convento de Santa Teresa, the smell
of iron on my hands, imagine the little beast
snapping awake to snatch the finger of the Saint of Avila

and run away with it as with a twig for the making of his nest.
I am no artist. I stood quietly before the narrow vase from which rose
her finger and yes, her fingernail, a single petal
clinging to the slender flaking stem which was bowed slightly as if
toward me. I leaned in to smell the heavenly
odor of sanctity, which is said to have sealed her sainthood
and scattered her arm, her heart, her finger. Did a honeysuckle
drift past on the air? I know only when the door opened to the light,
no holy spirit fell into attendance at my shoulders, no thump
of the white dove's wings. But soon I would dream
a tunnel blown through my heart, wake
hand in flight for my aching breast.

SIGHTSEER

If I linger a thousand years on this shore, I will become a shore crab
scurrying after the sea's parting embrace of this city. Already
the long arm of the estuary has begun to slip from this tiny island,
out from the shallows of which the Belém Tower bursts
like the brilliant underbelly of a Great White and its white
flash of jaw bedecked with spired trim.

Belém, pretty shark, time is a fisherman
who tangles his limestone rope in your balustrade.
How long has it been since ships heaved at the bastion
with sacks of cinnamon and nutmeg? Since your sentry posts
were wedged with men who wore the cupolas like helmets,
and rifles slid from your low embrasures like snakes wriggling into the sea?

The eyes of Our Lady of Safe Homecoming have turned to stone
from staring so long at stone over the terrace and into the empty sea.
In her prayers, she is a barnacle broken free by a passing boat,
a sightseer, the heavy Christ in her arms a bundle of souvenirs.
The velvety water rises to receive her steps. A silver flickering
in the moonlight, fish rushing to greet her ankles with their puffy lips.

DEAR PIGEONS, POLAND,

Thank you for being the only thing already at work
in the ten acres of pavement at Main Market Square

when all the shop windows were clicking their shades like tongues
and the Basilica of the Virgin Mary was shaking its gold plated crown

thinking *too early, too early*. No American woman
with a Nikon and a soft bag bulging at her back

should be walking here at such an hour in the morning
when the fog was still impaled on the Town Hall Tower

and had yet to rise off it like a wounded soldier
who rips the tough fruit of his own heart from the sword.

Thank you for letting me gawk at the Krakow I was not meant to see,
the vulnerable, slumbering Krakow whose infantry had yet to take its post

behind glass displays sprouting with green Polish amber,
and two-ply table-boards laid with rounds of lace

so torturously delicate you would have guessed the women
had taken their needles to a mound of snow, shaving a lean gauze

from where it settled, perfectly radial, on the head of a shrub.
Thank you for being so brave you didn't betray my silent infiltration

with a mad slapping of wings. For your puffed-out chests
and your bustling preoccupation with pecking at the ground, thank you.

Thank you for the obsessive neurosis of your seed-hunting dance,
in which you were like the wooden figurines of a cuckoo clock

who glide through the opening shutters in traditional Polish costume
(man in his black felt hat, woman in her silk vest embroidered with pearls)

and sweep their arc into the turning of the hour
as if they were skating on ice.

You were a hundred of these figurines
spilled onto the clockmaker's floor.

Thanks for your three-pronged hot pink feet
which seared into the frozen slabs of concrete,

for those lopsided stars of warmth as I shivered in my short sleeves
and vigorously rubbed the goose bumps from my arms.

As I slept bundled in the overnight train from Prague
I couldn't have known that the wheels' barreling down the tracks

was the force of the mercury sinking down the thermometer's
long slippery throat. When it was too early to buy a sweater

or even hot chocolate in a thin paper cup to press against my cheek,
thank you for being the one thing that reminded me of home.

Despite the fact that you are listed as one of the Tour Guide to Krakow's
Top Ten Must-See Landmarks, despite the fact

that you are so stalwart, so unflinching,
not even the brazen resounding bong of the Zygmunt bell's

660-pound clapper could send you off in a flurry,
that perhaps they are right to call you a landmark,

still you were no different from American pigeons
stabbing their beaks at the frozen slabs of concrete in Chicago.

You could have been New York City pigeons
deaf to the screeching of tires and horn honking,

going about that same crowded dance for the crumbs of a blueberry muffin
as if they had stolen from seagulls the secret of an ancient fisherman's knot

and were tying it there in Times Square.
You made me think of London, the pigeons in Trafalgar Square

gathering around the children who spilled seeds out of paper cones
that might as well have been dripping with ice cream.

They are the pigeons descended from pigeons
who heard the rumbling and shriek of the Blitz

and refused to scatter into exile, even as their delicate bones
were snapped by the hurling flight of bricks.

Neither the scampering torment of children's feet
nor the echo of Big Ben's distant alarm on the Thames

could lift those pigeons off the cement and into the trees.
Thank you for reminding me of my dearest friend

whom I photographed kneeling in that rippling flock,
holding out his hand as if he were touching the surface of a puddle.

I thought of the time we argued music theory late into the night
at the diner with the swivel-top bar stools and the plastic packets of cream,

and he leaned in, his long hair dipping into his Bottomless Cup O' Joe.
There's no such thing as a G scale, he whispered,

it's just the name someone gave to the sound of those seven notes
being played in that order. And with that, he puckered a kiss around his cigarette.

And suddenly when I looked around there were no swivel-top bar stools,
there was only the name we had for them. No plastic packets of cream.

The glasses that kept slipping down my friend's nose did not exist.
The finger he used to push them up again was not a finger.

That morning in Krakow, lonely and cold, you reminded me
that I *was* at home, that there is no such thing as Poland,

it is only the name someone gave to the shape the land makes
when it is drawn on a map, a leaf dangling out of the Baltic Sea.

Because there is no such thing as a Polish pigeon,
there must be no such thing as homesickness.

Thank you for reminding me of that moment I stepped outside
and took in with wide eyes the lamppost that didn't exist

and the light inside it that wasn't defining a fixed globe
through which the snowflakes flashed and then disappeared.

That was when I knew not everything could belong to me at once:
I could have either the entire world or language.

And as the heavy door of the diner swung shut behind me,
it latched with a sound so clamorous

it could have been the clapper of a giant bell
weighing six hundred and sixty pounds.

PRAYERS FOR A HEARSE

As I lie down to bed, let my room be darkened
with plush velvet drapes. The sterling silver cross hangs over my head.
Beside me in sleep, my lover makes a noise with his tongue—
the sharp clomp of a horseshoe on the street. If I sleep,
then at least let me dream of the hearse. Let me dream
that I swim in an ocean bobbing with hearses. Let butterflies
flitter with wings cast from the heavy steel of the hearse.
Oil lamps flicker in the windows like the eyes of a dead man
blinking away the disbelief of waking in the afterlife. I slip
the wallet from my pocket and the wallet becomes a matchbox
hearse in my palm, complete with miniature real-chrome hubcaps.
The lips of those who speak to me flap open like the doors of a hearse
in which is housed the moist, pink coffin. In the morning,
let my alarm be the wail of the police escort.
Fill my cereal bowl with hearses, so that I might start each day
with the crunch of the hearse between my teeth. How can I swallow
when the mucus is already evaporating from the throats of the newly dead?
How should I make it to the breakfast table? I should be stumbling,
if getting up at all, and if I manage my way to the bedroom door,
strike me to the ground, no holds barred. I deserve
to smack my temple hard on the doorknob on the way down.
And the carpet fibers, into which my cheek be forever smashed,
rougher than sand and gravel combined. Let me be forever stunned,
staring into the sideboard, that long white hearse.
Let me think of nothing but the heavy swarm of the dead
with which the earth is at any given moment slowly scintillating.

I want to be still, so still I become the single fixed center
the dead spin around in orbit.
I want to win the award for having lived
the least selfish life.

THE RUINS OF HOARE ABBEY

In the Golden Vale that ripples majestically beyond
your nameless field struts the Rock of Cashel built from
limestone which the devil bit from the mountain and
legend has it, spat back out in disgust, such was its nauseating
godliness. Who could hold a candle?

Little jagged thing, are you lonely for the hands of tourists
to smooth you down, for your share
of the moist *ooh*'s and *aah*'s that fog the King's clever twin towers?
In the evenings, do you watch the people descend
the paved road against the horizon like a dark millipede?

A prayer was chanted once in place of this vine
which now ascends the archway, dangling its flimsy bells.
Now only the grasshoppers ping through the leafy chapel.

What women are these buried in your yard
whose long hair has threaded the earth
and now waves its needles in the air?
The few who tread here bear an anklet of stings
to prove it.

Why so secretive? Is it the moss, wrapping its delicate
yellow gauze around your rubbled walls,
that binds your tongue?

I've seen the birds firecracker out your windows
in all directions, as if a great sigh
had blown them from their nests.

Tell me your story and I will retell it.
The tombstones stare from blank faces.
Sheep grind their teeth.

DEAR CAPE COD OYSTER,

All this time, we've been moving about the dim sand
pretending to be shadows, and you've been the one who's betrayed us,
your shells glaring like china plates slick in the tide.
With your sinewy hinge you open a window of light.
The geese squint. Beachcombers throw
their forearms over their eyes. How little
you understand. We long for a fog over the bay
like a curtain that billows into the room
and settles over the wooden chair,
over the head of the man sitting in the wooden chair,
listening to the wind rasp its breathy instrument against the house.
Oh, to be that suddenly shrouded, as a ghost
who was one moment a man and the next
invisible, afloat in the dissonant opus of death. Oyster,
in death, we are all that man sitting in his chair
with the newspaper in his lap, wrapped in a curtain.
A woman walks into the room, humming,
wiping her palm against her hip, and as she reaches with one hand
for the peg on the nightstand drawer, she turns the other wrist
and begins to sort-of kiss at the knuckle of her pinky finger.
Such exotic absentmindedness! In all these years
he has never seen, as he sees today (himself unseen)
through the tiny hollows in the curtain's weave,
this woman so intimately unconscious in her own body.
But when from the curtain comes a sudden throaty *oh*,
she drops her fist and turns to her husband.

Oyster, how little you understand of wanting to be invisible.
You, who lie on the beach, coughing up your blinding pearly white,
you must learn to be respectful of the dark. The dark
is why we come here so early in the morning.

ON THE WESTERN COAST OF ANGLESEY, THE TOURISTS

have come from the car park on the A4080
from London. They have already been
to the locked gate on the hill,
and peered into the mossy chamber
at the markings chipped into the rock
five thousand years ago, checked
if it were possible to see
through the shadows
human bones, which it wasn't.

In their little books, they read about
ashes in the southern chamber, and in the
central hearth the charred remains of the vigil
meal, from which is revealed
a lot about the life of ancient man.

But now the women have lowered themselves
from the hill to the bay, and stand on the sand
among the cold pebbles which stare like the dead
whose eyelids have rinsed away.
The water rushes over them and recedes.
The burial mound is nothing more than
a hump of grass on the hill.

One woman holds the camera. In the wind,
the women's hair is a mass of arms
waving in triumph. *Goodbye remains, five-thousand-year-old
eels, goodbye vertebrae, blackened snakes and frogs and
mouse tails, goodbye.*

The women switch places. They are alive. They stand
on the pebbles in their hiking boots.

THE WINDING STAIR

If there is a shell pulled from the shallow
muddy waters of the Indian Ocean
they call the Winding Stair,
I have found its sister shells
radiating the cloister
at the Convento de Cristo de Tomar.

Each stairwell scooped
slick of its spongy mollusk. What a feast
must have contented the architect
whose workers dragged their giant
spoons to his table! Airy spines
flushed with light, so one might
ascend in the creamy
dizzying rapture of Christ.

Is it the ocean
he hoped the monks would hear
as their tatters swished against
the marble conch? And what was it
I listened for? A scrap of prayer, the horse's
impatient snort, his clacking shoe
chiming still within the rotunda
where once the knights sat
mass in their dingy saddles,
where hung the *Resurrection*,
the *Ascension*?

A voice to rise through the Gothic
cemetery's crooked teeth, where it has
pressed for many years against the earth?
With only a cough the hour passes,
the rush of wings, an ordinary
startled sparrow and his flock.

Nearby, the great window
looks out upon the terrace
through its monocle of coral and seaweed.

And no one tells me
if this is the year
the festival returns to Tomar,
the one in which a girl carries a tray upon her head
prepared with bread and flowers.
The apparition of her white gown.

RACE POINT BEACH

This is the duneland: shifting heaps
marked here and there by a twiggy growth. Slumped against a ridge,

a dune shack wound in a snarl of fencing, wooden slats
the darkened jagged bones of some unknowable animal

long since suffocated by sand. The ocean
is the voice in my head that will never cease.

The crunch of a seagull's flat feet like a boot in the snow.
And then there is the racket the crickets make in the pits.

I am the woman standing alone in the middle of nowhere, the tall pale thing
pinking like a rose. If I were to collapse here, in this very spot,

what creature scurrying through the sand on its claws
bright and sharp as sharks' teeth would find me?

The husk of some crustacean washed up on the shore. A kite
in the distance like a lemon drop dangling in the sky.

THE HIGHLAND COW

When at night I rise and cross the wooden floor
to greet the brilliance at my window, the darkness
of my heart spills behind me like the train of an evening
gown, a vaguely human form. In this moon
I recognize the eye of a great beast emerging
from the grasses. Ten years pass
as she makes her way across the moor,
her line of sight whipped open and closed again
behind her forelock tossed by the teasing hands
of ocean winds. She lifts her chin to the fencepost, eye
like the slowly swirling atmosphere of a planet
viewed from a distance, and all the darkness inside me
illuminated. The delicate blossom clings
to the heather. Was I meant to move my hand
into the path of her hot breath
just as it was wrenched away across the heath?
One horn pointing east and to the sky. The other
west and to the sky. The windowsill
is damp. In the distance, a smokestack surges forth,
a fat grey worm wriggling at the heavens.
A cluster of sweetly fragranced bells
chimes softly from the corner of my room.

DEAR BED, APARTMENT C,

Since I am already prostrate, and accustomed
to pressing my forehead to your pillowy darkness
as if to a gently forgiving earth, or otherwise
staring deep into the ceiling of heaven, I should confess
the entire summer and every sparrow that attended my feet,
two ghostly stumps, the chirp of the neighbors' car alarms
disengaged at dawn, and at dusk, in a flock, engaged again. I confess loss
of energy, the sweat of sleeping, extreme negativity
or brooding, the trouble with leaving you.
But I cannot be held accountable for cotton or the bounce
with which you champion my dramatic and childish flailings,
to which I also now confess. You belong to the diaspora of beds
in silent exile across the nation, each hidden away, shamefaced,
in its own dark room, beds which let us collapse
into them drunk or in despair and ask no questions.
Spasi menya, krovat moya. Save me, O my bed.
Muster the strength of your 704 coil springs, pop them
right through your padded top quilt, shove me out the apartment
door, back to Russia, back to the Nevsky Monastery
at the hour of vespers when the monks gather in the cathedral
like movie stars at a cocktail party, and the twilight
speckles their shaved heads with bits of the savior's stained-glass coat,
and both of us will be absolved. In the Tikhvin Cemetery,
even the dead can't sleep. Deep in the Trinity Cathedral,

where vibrantly woven rugs ascend three steps to the shrine,
and cherubim cast in silver flap their wings,
the relics of Saint Alexander Nevsky
knock around in the glass case like jumping beans.

THE SECOND LARGEST WOODEN CUPOLA IN EUROPE BURNS

The Troitsky Cathedral is a white spider
towering on her classical white legs. She carries
her young on her back, a little cluster of domes.
Look, she sputters a trail of smoke. I am not
in St. Petersburg anymore. The rain
carries on its seventh day. Flowers bow their heads.
Here, the purple-hooded monks. Here,
the many-fingered hands clasped in prayer.
Now that the Troitsky Cathedral burns, I sit
at my desk, of all things, a poet. Even
in Wisconsin, I cannot rid my garden
of the white spider. The ghost of Dostoyevsky
kneeling at the altar with his young bride. The
worms chewing at the bindings of the Gospel.
At night, the path to my porch is the long silver cross.
Look for me, you will find my house
by the flickering blaze that creeps among
the grass.

Acknowledgments

Grateful acknowledgment is made to the publications in which the following poems first appeared, sometimes in previous versions or with different titles:

Crab Orchard Review: "Burning Paper in Lazarus Cemetery"; "The Heart of Sintra"
Connections: "Dear Athassel Priory,"
Elixir: "The Winding Stair"
The George Washington Review: "Dear Bed, Apartment C,"
Fourteen Hills: "Dear Cape Cod Oyster,"; "Dear Herzen Inn,"
Margie: "Dear Remu'h Synagogue,"
New Delta Review: "Dear Florescent Pink Jumbo Finger Starfish,"
Nimrod: "Sheepification"
Pebble Lake Review: "Tomb"
Phoebe: "Dear Alexander Nevsky,"

"Dear Alexander Nevsky," was reprinted in the anthology *Best New Poets 2005: 50 Poems from Emerging Writers*.

With deep gratitude to my mentors Carolyn Forché, Jennifer Atkinson, and Eric Pankey, and for the MFA program at George Mason University. Thanks to Diane Middlebrook and the Wisconsin Institute for Creative Writing, and to Sandra Gilbert and the Summer Literary Seminars in St. Petersburg, Russia. With appreciation to Gabriel Fried, Persea Books, and the Lexi Rudnitsky Poetry Project. To the fellow poets and friends who read and critiqued these poems. And to my mother and father, Diane and William Hoffman.

The Lexi Rudnitsky First Book Prize in Poetry

The Lexi Rudnitsky First Book Prize in Poetry (formerly the Lexi Rudnistky Poetry Prize) is a collaboration between Persea Books and The Lexi Rudnitsky Poetry Project. It sponsors the annual publication of a poetry collection by an American woman who has yet to publish a full-length book of poems. Lexi Rudnitsky (1972–2005) grew up outside of Boston. She studied at Brown University and Columbia University, where she wrote poetry and cultivated a profound relationship with a lineage of women poets that extends from Muriel Rukeyser to Heather McHugh. Her own poems exhibit both a playful love of language and a fierce conscience. Her writing appeared in *The Antioch Review, Columbia: A Journal of Literature and Art, The Nation, The New Yorker, The Paris Review, Pequod*, and *The Western Humanities Review*. In 2004, she won the Milton Kessler Memorial Prize for Poetry from Harpur Palate. Lexi died suddenly in 2005, just months after the birth of her first child and the acceptance for publication of her first book of poems, *A Doorless Knocking into Night* (Mid-List Press, 2006). The Lexi Rudnitsky Poetry Prize was founded to memorialize her and to promote the type of poet and poetry in which she so spiritedly believed.

Previous winners of the Lexi Rudnitsky First Book Prize in Poetry:

> 2009 Alexandra Teague, *Mortal Geography*
> 2008 Tara Bray, *Mistaken for Song*
> 2007 Anne Shaw, *Undertow*
> 2006 Alena Hairston, *The Logan Topographies*